ASIAPAC CULTURE

Origins of
CHINESE
MARTIAL ARTS

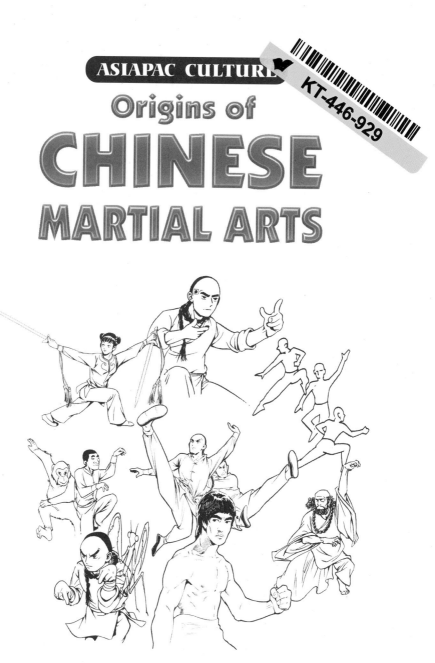

Illustrated by Jack Cheong   Translated by Laurel Teo
Editorial consultant: Loh Chong Chai

⚭ ASIAPAC • SINGAPORE

Publisher
ASIAPAC BOOKS PTE LTD
996 Bendemeer Road #06-09
Singapore 339944
Tel: (65) 6392 8455
Fax: (65) 6392 6455
Email: asiapacbooks@pacific.net.sg

Come visit us at our Internet home page
www.asiapacbooks.com

First published June 2002
6th edition (revised) April 2007

© 2002 ASIAPAC BOOKS, SINGAPORE
ISBN 981-229-268-3

Cover illustrations by Jack Cheong
Cover design by Kelly Lim
Body text in 11pt Times New Roman
Printed in Singapore by FuIsland Offset Printing (S) Pte Ltd

Publisher's Note

Thanks to an endless slew of martial-art flicks, including the internationally-acclaimed *Crouching Tiger, Hidden Dragon*, and the timeless appeal of martial-art novels like *The Legend of the Condor Heroes*, interest in Chinese martial arts is kept alive.

The worldwide fascination with martial arts has led to the proliferation of martial-art schools all over the world. For example, the Northern Shaolin Martial Arts Academy in northern China takes in both male and female lay students and teaches them traditional Shaolin *qigong* and real *gongfu*.

In this volume, readers can learn about the origins of Chinese martial arts, established institutions like Shaolin and Wudang, martial-art experts like Zhang Sanfeng and Bruce Lee, the various boxing and weapon arts, as well as the ethics underlying martial arts.

We would like to take this opportunity to thank Jack Cheong for his illustrations, Laurel Teo for her translation and *Taiji* instructor Loh Chong Chai for sharing with us his valuable knowledge. Our appreciation, too, to the production team for their best efforts in putting this book together.

Latest in the Culture Series:

ORIGINS OF CHINESE NAMES
Find out the origins of 100 Chinese family names, and understand how names are chosen. It may fascinate you to know that Chinese family names have a history of five or six thousand years, whilst given names are not chosen randomly but reflect the customs and beliefs of the times.

Preface to the Chinese Culture Series

Tens of thousands of years ago, the eastern part of the northern hemisphere was a wide expanse of land which was populated by a group of people. They learnt to gather wood and make fires. They started to hunt, fish and farm. They invented written text. They created culture. They established a nation.

They were the earliest Huaxia people who prospered and multiplied to become the largest ethnic group on Earth. They developed by leaps and bounds to forge a dazzling culture. Many a brilliant ancient civilisation has been swallowed up by the currents of time, but the Huaxia culture has managed to survive. In fact, it continues to exert its influence today, not only within China, but also without, via the Silk Road, migration, etc.

The flames of wars erupted. Dynasties rose and fell. Despite the changing faces of political power, the essence of the Chinese people has remained unchanged.

Today, the Chinese people are not merely an ethnic group, but a larger cultural entity spread all over the world.

The most distinguishing aspect of Chinese culture is its all-encompassing nature. It emphasises justice and moral integrity, human relations, the power of music and rituals to cultivate the hearts of men, and the oneness of Man and Heaven... all at the same time. Next is its wisdom — it engineers invention and change, and is prolific and dynamic. Last but not least is its ingenuity — it is ever progressive and enlightening.

Taking a flying leap into the global lake of the world, the ancient Chinese culture exudes the vitality of youth!

Li Xiaoxiang

About the Illustrator

Jack Cheong 张开振 graduated from the Malaysia Institute of Art. Driven by his passion for comics, he entered the field of comics in 1995.

Having worked as an assistant to various cartoonists in Singapore and Malaysia, he has built up a wide repertoire that includes period, modern and sci-fi comics. Currently a freelancer, he also creates animation for websites.

Asiapac Books' *Origins of Chinese Martial Arts* is his very first solo effort. His bestselling works also include *Top Crime Busters* and *Origins of Shaolin Kung Fu*.

He can be reached at zplace2000@yahoo.com.

Contents

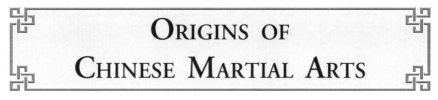
The Chinese martial arts (*wushu* 武术) that is known throughout the Eastern and Western worlds is an exotic branch of traditional Chinese culture. Its contents are rich, encompassing boxing and weapon arts. It is also divided into different schools and styles. Exuding power and grace in its execution, it stands out in a class of its own from other fighting arts.

The *wu* 武 character is formed from the words *ge* 戈 and *zhi* 止. *Ge* refers to a kind of weapon. It is also a general term for arms and weaponry. In ancient writing, *zhi* is a hieroglyph for the foot, and it means to advance or march forward.

Hence, *wu* means to take up arms and advance, that is to *dongwu* 动武 (use force or come to blows). Later on, it was also extended to mean brave, bold, tough and forceful.

Chinese martial arts is the origin of all other martial arts in the world. But when did Chinese martial arts itself emerge? And under what sort of circumstances?

This can be traced back to the prehistoric era...

At that time, there were very few human beings. They had to contend with many wild beasts prowling the Earth, and were often attacked by the animals.

Gradually, Man developed a few defensive and offensive moves.

This simplest and most direct primitive *wushu* was the embryonic form of Chinese martial arts. Later on, when human society kept expanding, tribes and villages appeared.

Ancient Forms of the Word *Dou* 斗.

In ancient writing, the word *dou* — which means to fight — resembles two people entangled in a fist-fight, exchanging slaps and punches. This earliest kind of fighting was the embryonic form of the boxing arts (unarmed combat).

Long
spear

Stone
knife

Stone axe

Wooden pike

Stone mallet

Wooden cudgel

Bone arrowhead

The brawls between humans were much more complex than their struggles with animals, and resulted in the invention and improvement of even more weapons.

Chinese martial arts was thus born of the need to fight off wild beasts and human enemies.

The Characteristics of Chinese Martial Arts

Chinese martial arts has absorbed the essence of ancient Chinese philosophy and aesthetics, culminating in the distinct features of "Heaven and Man as one" (*tian ren he yi* 天人合一), and "beauty in form and spirit" (*xing shen jian mei* 形神兼美).

Heaven and Man as one
Experts in Chinese martial arts believe that Heaven, Earth and Man are intimately connected. So for a person's training to achieve maximum effect, he must comply with the changes and movements of celestial bodies. The ancients used to retreat to a still and secluded forest, mountain or temple to practise their arts, or would practise different routines according to different seasons. These were all expressions of "Heaven and Man as one".

Beauty in form and spirit
Chinese aesthetics places a premium on form and spirit. For instance, in portrait painting, not just the physical likeness but the subject's moods and expressions must be captured as well, before the portrait can be considered a masterpiece. The same applies to martial arts. Beautiful postures alone may be eye-pleasing, but are meaningless. One must still cultivate the inner essence (*jing* 精), vital energy or life force (*qi* 气) and spirit (*shen* 神), before one can truly master the quintessence of Chinese martial arts. That is why martial-art exponents have this saying: "To work the muscle, sinew and bone externally, and to build up the life force internally."

The Mystique of
Chinese Martial Arts

Those of us familiar with Chinese martial-art shows or novels must be truly impressed by their descriptions of Acupoint Tapping and gravity-defying Light Skills. Were there truly people who had mastered such mystical skills in the history of Chinese martial arts? Or were they merely figments of the fantastic imaginations of script-writers or novelists?

Acupoint Tapping

In martial-art movies, we often see a highly-skilled exponent tapping a spot on his opponent's body, rendering the victim motionless — sometimes even speechless — in the blink of an eye. This mysterious skill is known as Acupoint Tapping (*dianxue* 点穴).

An acupoint, or acupuncture point, is a specific location on the human body where there is a dense gathering of nerve ends, or where a particularly thick nerve lies. If one suffers an injury at a key acupoint, it would lead to blood stasis*, paralysing that part of the body or the entire person, and may even lead to death.

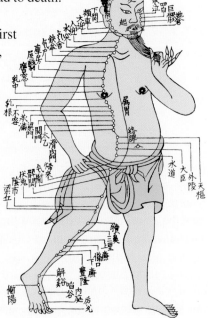

To execute Acupoint Tapping, one must first exert one's internal force (*neili* 内力), directing energy flow to the hand, finger or palm, and then using either a tap of the finger, a slap or a punch, to check the opponent's acupuncture points and passages. Although Acupoint Tapping is plausible in theory, it is tricky to carry out in actuality, because in combat, it is extremely difficult to pin down the opponent's exact acupoint. Nonetheless, it is still useful to understand the layout of acupuncture points and passages throughout the human body, as one can then protect one's own key points from attacks.

---

* Blood which is not moving properly, but is stagnating or even clotting.

Light Skills

Light Skills (*qinggong* 轻功) refer to specific martial-art methods and techniques that train the body to be light and nimble. The *qinggong* that approximates to flying as depicted in movies and novels stems from writers' exaggerated and stylised interpretations.

In Shaolin *gongfu* 功夫, there are different types of *qinggong*, such as "Lizard gliding on wall" and "Flying on eaves and walking on walls". But these are all consummate skills that require years of painstaking practice. Few can attain such skills.

Ancients also relied on their surroundings or tools to help them achieve a certain level of proficiency in jumping and leaping. For instance, ancient walls were made of mud and stone and had many bumps and cracks, so it was possible to find footholds on these walls and climb up, step by step. Ancients also wore belts up to four metres long, which could be used as ropes to help them swing and fly.

Diamond Armour and Diamond Finger

There is a type of *gongfu* called "Diamond Armour" (*jingang zhao* 金刚罩), in which the chest and back are trained to be as firm as metal and stone, and the arms and legs to be impervious to knife or sword stabbings. However, one must endure repeated blows from wooden and metal hammers during the training process. Without steely determination and a strong physique, it would be impossible to attain such a skill.

An expert in the powerful "Diamond Finger" (*jingang zhi* 金刚指) skill could bore holes in wooden blocks and shatter stones with just a stab of the finger. Training entails using the forefinger to stab repeatedly at walls, trees and other hard surfaces day and night. Initially, there is no need to exert too much force. But as time progresses, one increases the pressure in each stab. After several years of practice, one would be able to master the skill.

Internal exercises and the danger of straying down demonic paths

In *gongfu* movies, characters often train rigorously in isolation. If they use the wrong training methods, or are interrupted halfway through the training process, they could well be thrown off and "stray down the demonic path" (*zouhuo rumo* 走火入魔) instead. In mild cases, they merely suffer paralysis; in severe cases, they would vomit blood and die. What does it mean to "stray down the demonic path"? This is where internal exercises come into play.

Internal exercise (*neigong* 内功) refers to the training a person undertakes to control his stream of *qi* 气* — vital energy or life force — such that it flows continuously and smoothly. Most ordinary people inhale about 18 breaths per minute, but skilled people can survive on as few as three. From the scientific viewpoint, people who inhale less frequently have healthier hearts and lungs, and better stamina. Experts in *neigong* can control their breath and vital energy flow with ease. They can also focus their entire body's strength into their every punch and kick.

It is crucial to follow the correct procedure in exercising the vital energy. One must never hurry or rush, and should also assume the correct posture or position. Otherwise, blood and vital energy would go into stasis. Not only would this be harmful to health, it may even result in paralysis. This is the so-called "straying down the demonic path".

Oops! I've strayed down the demonic path!

Concentrating *Qi* in *Dantian*

Dantian 丹田 is an acupoint located three inches below the navel. "Concentrating *qi* in *dantian*" refers to the practice of abdominal breathing during martial-art training. Using sheer will, one guides the flow of breathing, as if one were drawing breath deep down into the *dantian*. This is the first step towards exercising *qi*. Once a person masters this skill, he can control and direct his *qi* flow to any part of the body.

The word qi is written with the character that usually means "air," "breath," or even "steam." But this is only the outer, external breath. The word qi is used by practitioners of martial arts to mean "internal prana", life force, vital energy or biopsychic internal energy.

SCHOOLS OF MARTIAL ARTS

There are many schools of Chinese martial arts, the most famous of which are Shaolin and Wudang.

Shaolin and Wudang each has its unique characteristics. They are the leading representatives of external exercises and internal exercises respectively. Shaolin *gongfu* focusses on strengthening muscles and bones, through rapid and powerful moves. Wudang *gongfu*, on the other hand, stresses cultivating *qi*; its movements are gentle, and tend towards using inertia to conquer movement.

The Story of Shaolin

Throughout history, there is a saying that "all Chinese martial arts stem from Shaolin". Although it may not be strictly accurate, nonetheless, it is an indication of the unrivalled position that Shaolin holds in the world of martial arts. And for this reason, the fame of Shaolin Monastery has spread far beyond its home in the Song mountains (Songshan 嵩山). This historical ground, located in central China's He'nan Province, Dengfeng County, has become a mecca for both Eastern and Western martial-art lovers. The history of Shaolin Monastery (also known as Shaolin Temple) goes back for 1,500 years. Built by Emperor Xiao Wen in AD 495 during the Northern Wei era, it was meant to house visiting monks from India.

A treasure trove of martial arts

Most of the monks in Shaolin Monastery were commoners. Some of them were already well-versed in martial arts before they joined the order. And when they entered the monastery, they exchanged their *wushu* skills. Gradually, the monastic order built up a vast collection of different types of *wushu*, giving rise to the saying "All Chinese martial arts stem from Shaolin."

Throughout the order's history, the abbots have also encouraged their warrior monks to travel out of the monastery and visit *gongfu* experts around the country, gleaning the essence of different schools of martial arts from the various regions. By adopting and encompassing such a broad range of strengths, Shaolin *gongfu* managed to grow and flourish throughout its long history.

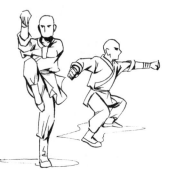

Bodhidharma and Shaolin

Legend has it that Shaolin *wushu* was founded during the Southern Dynasties — in AD520 — by a Buddhist monk from India called Bodhidharma (Damo 达摩). Based on the distinctive characteristics and movements of various wild animals, he created a set of exercises to work out muscles and joints. From then on, it became a custom for Shaolin monks to practise martial arts as a way of keeping fit.

The story of how Bodhidharma founded Shaolin *wushu* is considered a myth by many. According to textual research, even before the arrival of Bodhidharma, monks in many temples and monasteries had begun to practise martial arts quite intensely. This was because religion was encouraged right at the start of the Northern Wei era. As the power and influence of Buddhist institutions grew steadily, monks begun to practise combat skills secretly within their compounds. They were preparing to overthrow the Northern Wei rulers, who were Xianbei (鲜卑*) people. Later on, the Northern Wei rulers began to suppress Buddhism, banning the monks from practising combat skills. The monks then turned martial arts into a form of post-meal exercises to aid digestion.

As one of the major religious institutions in the land, Shaolin was wealthy. Legend has it that the monastery had a set of eight arhat statues cast in solid gold. Naturally, robbers and plunderers began casting their greedy eyes on the rumoured riches. So most monks picked up martial arts as a form of self-defence. In fact, in the early years, their skills and techniques probably originated from the public at large, before they developed a school of their own. As for whether Bodhidharma ever practised any martial arts, that remains a mystery.

Achoo! Someone's talking about me behind my back...

*The Xianbei are a Tungusic tribe originating from the plains of what is now Siberia, Manchuria and eastern Mongolia.

Characteristics of Shaolin Boxing

According to legend, Shaolin Boxing, or Shaolin *Quan* 少林拳, encompasses 172 routines (excluding the weapon arts). The monastery also had boxing instruction manuals carved onto wood, and had them displayed in the main hall. The inner hall was for the exclusive use of martial-art practice, and was equipped with racks of assorted weapons ready for use. There were also some monks who were specially trained to protect the monastery.

Shaolin Boxing is the leading representative of external boxing skills. The external school places emphasis on strengthening muscle and bone. Its strengths include powerful moves and swift counterblows. In fact, "Shaolin Boxing" is a loose term for all the various boxing skills practised in the vicinity of Shaolin. There are more than 50 types, including Big Flood Boxing, Little Flood Boxing, Arhat Boxing, Plum Blossom Boxing, Seven-Star Boxing, and the Five Boxing Arts of Shaolin, and so on.

"Fist strikes out in a straight line" is the clearest feature of Shaolin Boxing. Routines in this school tend to be short and simple, with straightforward moves.

It takes tremendous effort to master Shaolin Boxing. For instance, it takes at least three years to get the basics — such as standing postures — right. And another "three years of suspending arms, three years of sticking to walls" are spent learning to sleep with both arms suspending from a roof beam, or while clinging to a wooden pillar against the wall. There is also sandbag punching — three years of stabbing at bags filled with peas, before moving onto sand.

Without a steely determination and perseverance, mastering Shaolin Boxing would be near impossible.

The Northern and Southern Shaolins
(***nanbei Shaolin*** 南北少林)

Besides the Shaolin of Song mountains, there was also a Southern Shaolin Monastery. At the dawn of the Qing Dynasty, some Shaolin disciples set up a branch in the southern province of Fujian. To distinguish between the new Shaolin in Fujian and the original one in the Song mountains, people came up with the names of Southern/Northern Shaolin.

Later, Ming* loyalists infiltrated the southern order, spreading anti-Qing ideology within the monastery. At that time, lamas** wielded great power and might, and were often embroiled in disputes with the Buddhist monasteries. In the end, the lamas teamed up with the Qing officials and set Southern Shaolin aflame.

The only Shaolin monk who escaped alive was Zhi Wu (至悟), a senior fellow-disciple of the abbot Zhi Shan (至善). He subsequently taught all his martial skills to a layman called Cai Jiuyi (蔡九仪). When Zhi Wu's life ended, so did the monastic order of Southern Shaolin. And Cai Jiuyi became the first-generation leader of Shaolin's "secular order". Thereafter, the Southern Shaolin branch passed into the secular realm among the common folk.

Shaolin on fire
The Shaolin of the Song mountains suffered a similar fate. It was set on fire by warlord Shi Yousan during the Nationalist Republic era. The fire raged on for over 40 days, destroying the main halls and temples. Many secret medical and martial-art manuals were also burnt to cinders along with the scripture library.

---

*The Ming Dynasty was overthrown by Manchurian invaders, who named their new dynasty "Qing".
**Lamaism refers to Tibetan Buddhism, which is different from the Mahayana Buddhism practised among most Chinese Buddhists today.

On the way there, Bodhidharma came upon the Yangtze River. He wanted to cross over to the northern bank, but there was no boat in sight.

Bodhidharma plucked a reed and crossed the Yangtze River on it.

For nine years, Bodhidharma sat meditating in the cave, facing the walls. Besides Snake Boxing and Crane Boxing, he also created the Dragon, Tiger and Leopard Boxing skills. Together, the exercises were known as the Five Boxing Arts of Shaolin.

He returned to the monastery, where he passed on his new-found skills to the monks.

The monks grew strong and fit with these exercises. No longer did they tire so easily when they meditated.

From then on, it became a tradition at Shaolin Monastery to practise martial arts. The fame of Shaolin *wushu* spread far and wide thereafter. And Bodhidharma naturally became known as the founding father of orthodox Chinese martial arts.

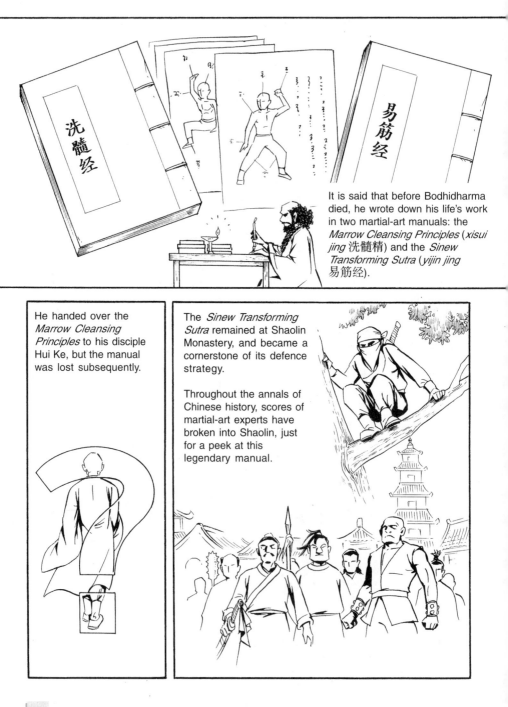

It is said that before Bodhidharma died, he wrote down his life's work in two martial-art manuals: the *Marrow Cleansing Principles* (*xisui jing* 洗髓精) and the *Sinew Transforming Sutra* (*yijin jing* 易筋经).

He handed over the *Marrow Cleansing Principles* to his disciple Hui Ke, but the manual was lost subsequently.

The *Sinew Transforming Sutra* remained at Shaolin Monastery, and became a cornerstone of its defence strategy.

Throughout the annals of Chinese history, scores of martial-art experts have broken into Shaolin, just for a peek at this legendary manual.

Ji Guang and Bodhidharma

Huff!

Puff!

Once there was a man named Ji Guang (姬光). He had been frail and weakly for as long as anyone could remember. Even when he reached the age of 25, he was still too weak to carry an ordinary load of water.

A formidable Indian monk has arrived at Songshan Shaolin!

He's not just an expert in Buddhist doctrine. He's also devised a set of strengthening exercises.

That's right! Now every Shaolin monk is strong and fit, and skilled in martial arts too.

When Ji Guang heard that, he decided to seek out Bodhidharma and become his disciple. He arrived at the sage's rock cave at Wuru Peak. Bodhidharma happened to be practising his skills.

After a long bout of practice, Bodhidharma returned to his cave and sat down, facing the wall. Ji Guang hurried in after him...

Wordlessly, Ji Guang took out a dagger...

Religious studies require twice as much effort as martial-art practice. Do you have what it takes?

...and hacked off his right arm.

All right! I bestow upon you the religious name of Hui Ke (慧可). You are now officially the second-generation follower of the *Chan* sect.

How Jue Min Learnt His Skills

During the Northern Song Dynasty, there was a little monk at Shaolin. His name was Jue Min and he yearned with all his heart to learn martial arts.

Master, please teach me some skills!

All right, but first, go get me a fly. Remember! I want it alive!

But...

With that, his mentor handed him a pair of iron chopsticks.

What does Master want with a fly? And how can I possibly catch it with a pair of chopsticks?

Bapp!

Bapp!

The fly was tiny, and it zipped around speedily. Every day and night, Jue Min tried clamping one from the air. Thus a whole year came and went.

Master! Master! I caught a fly!

Go catch another year of flies!

Crestfallen, Jue Min resumed his fly-catching exercise.

One day, as he swung out his hand unthinkingly, he pinched a fly right in mid-flight. He tried a couple more times, and succeeded with the same ease.

Ha, ha! I did it! Master! Master!

While the enemy was not paying attention, Jue Min climbed to the top of the gate.

Huh?

And as the enemy arrows came flying towards him, he raised his pair of iron chopsticks and started plucking them from mid-air, as if they were flying insects.

In a short while, he had collected two large piles of arrows.

The Story of Wudang

Rising from Jun County in the north-western parts of Hubei Province are the Wudang mountains. Not only is the mountain range a scenic spot, it is also the sacred grounds of one of China's oldest religions — Taoism. And throughout the history of Chinese martial arts, only the Taoist Wudang Sect could match Buddhist Shaolin in terms of strength and standing.

The Wudang school puts emphasis on cultivating *qi*, which basically means to build up internal strength. This focus is directly related to Taoism's concern about deep breathing and preserving health, and even prolonging life. Legend has it that the Wudang Sect was founded during the Ming Dynasty, by a Taoist priest named Zhang Sanfeng 张三丰.

Zhang Sanfeng the scruffy priest

Zhang Sanfeng was born in the twilight of the Yuan Dynasty and dawn of the Ming Dynasty. According to legend, he cut a very strange figure: he stooped like a tortoise, had spindly limbs like those of a stork, and long, rapier-thin moustaches. His unkempt appearance earned him the nickname of "Scruffy Zhang". He wore a heavily-patched robe all through summer and winter, and was never seen without a wide-brimmed bamboo hat perched on his head.

His habits were very odd. If he went on the move, he would travel 1,000 *li* 里 (about 500 km) in a day. But if he was inclined to be still, he could close his eyes for 10 days at a stretch. Whenever he ate or drank, he would gulp down gallons of food. Yet at other times, he would go without a bite or a sip for days or even months on end, and still seemed perfectly fine. He chortled with joy and roared with anger on a whim, without giving two hoots about what others might think.

In the last days of the Yuan Dynasty, he lived at the Golden Rooster Shrine, and died while meditating in a lotus position. Hs good pal Yang Guishan ordered a coffin for him. But as Yang was about to lay the corpse into the coffin, Zhang Sanfeng opened his eyes wide and leapt up.

Following his resurrection, Zhang left for the Wudang mountains and lived there for another 23 years, gathering disciples to set up the Wudang Sect. Then he took off to roam the world, coming and going mysteriously like a phantom, without a trace.

During the Yongle reign of the Ming Dynasty, the imperial court erected a monument in his memory. Subsequently during the Tianshun reign, he was awarded the title of the "Enlightened and Illustrious Immortal".

Zhang Sanfeng as a Youth

Zhang Sanfeng entered Shaolin Monastery at a tender age, and earned his keep doing odd jobs in the kitchen.

There was a master stoker* in the kitchen, who turned out to be a *gongfu* virtuoso as well.

Wow! That was incredible!

Would you like to learn to do that?

But that was so amazing! Could I ever do that?

It's not too difficult to master, but you can't do it overnight. If you have the patience and determination, I don't mind teaching you. But you have to keep our lessons a secret.

My respects to Master!

Good!

A stoker tends to a furnace by feeding it with fuel.

He had flung the monk across the entire courtyard!

Argh!

Huh? Since when did I become so powerful?

Who taught you martial arts!

I don't know any martial arts...

I just flung my arms, then he flew into the air and landed so far away...

Heh!

Abbot...

Have mercy on me, Abbot!

It's true that you don't have any combat skills. But how did you build up so much internal strength?

Who taught you? You have stolen our skills — that makes you guilty of deception! Such behaviour cannot be condoned under our monastery's rules!

Make way!
Make way!

Ah!

The master stoker stuffed Zhang Sanfeng into a bucket and charged down the mountain without pausing.

Master, it's all my fault! I got you into trouble!

He sat down and pondered deeply, going over the idea again and again in his mind. His efforts finally culminated in the *Taiji* shadow boxing.

This school of shadow boxing puts emphasis on exercising the *qi* through all body passages, using the soft to counter the firm, and inertia to conquer movement.

The enlightened Zhang Sanfeng began passing on his skills to disciples in the Wudang mountains, where he founded the Wudang Sect.

Taiji Shadow Boxing

Taiji Shadow Boxing, or *Taiji Quan* 太极拳, is the leading representative of the internal school of boxing. Internal *quan* or shadow boxing focusses on cultivating *qi*, and is characterised by soft and gentle moves, using inertia to conquer movement.

Yin

In ancient philosophy, *Taiji*, which means the Supreme Ultimate, is the source from which all creatures in the universe spring forth. It is divided into two opposing forces of *yin* (dark, negative, feminine) and *yang* (light, positive, masculine).

The *Taiji* diagram (cosmological scheme) is a circle, so each and every move in *Taiji* shadow boxing is also circular.

Yang

The moves are divided into big circles, small circles, semi-circles, ovals, arcs and spirals. From the first move to the end of the exercise routine, all the loops are closely linked, flowing smoothly from one into another, and executed with perfect grace and beauty.

Taiji is the motive force behind all the changes in the universe. In the human body, the motive force is also located at the *Taiji* point (abdomen). Hence in *Taiji* Shadow Boxing, all movements are triggered by the movement of the abdominal muscles, radiating to the rest of the body. Once the abdominal muscles (*Taiji*) move, the rest of the body is led into motion as well.

The practice of *Taiji Quan* emphasises:

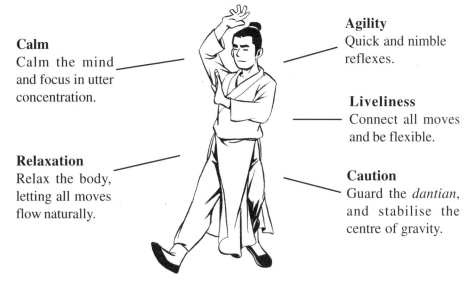

Calm
Calm the mind and focus in utter concentration.

Relaxation
Relax the body, letting all moves flow naturally.

Agility
Quick and nimble reflexes.

Liveliness
Connect all moves and be flexible.

Caution
Guard the *dantian*, and stabilise the centre of gravity.

Taiji Quan moves are gentle and slow. They can be used either in pugilistic duels and performances, or as an exercise to strengthen the body's consititution and prevent, even cure, ailments. They are suitable for the elderly or the frail.

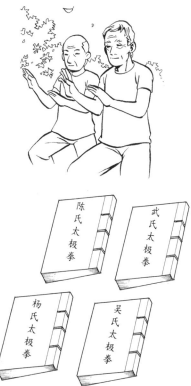

Legend has it that *Taiji Quan* was created by Zhang Sanfeng, the founding patriarch of Wudang Sect. Subsequently, *Taiji Quan* split into the four main schools of Chen-style 陈氏, Wu-style 武氏, Yang-style 杨氏 and Wu-style 吴氏.

At present, the most popular version is the Yang-style *Taiji* Shadow Boxing, founded by Yang Luchan during the Qing Dynasty. The Yang-style moves are clean and simple, and thus more accessible to the wider public.

Thus each night, Yang Luchan crouched outside the wall and peeped at the training sessions. Then secretly, he would practise the stolen moves over and over again.

One day, Yang Luchan had a dispute with a big and burly servant.

What? You want a fight, Shortie? Come on!

Without thinking, Yang Luchan unwittingly used *Taiji Quan* moves to defeat his strapping opponent.

How dare you! Who taught you our Chen-style **Taiji Quan** moves?

Master Chen, please forgive me!

I couldn't get you to teach me, so I learnt the moves on my own...

Good! Very good! You have great potential! With proper training, I have no doubt that you will be a shining star in the future!

All right, I'll make an exception and accept you as my disciple. I'll teach you all that I know about Taiji Quan.

Thank you Master, thank you!

When Yang Luchan's training was complete, he left the Chen household to test his skills in Beijing.

There, the slightly-built man triumphed over a whole string of renowned fighters who were much taller and heftier.

His fame spread throughout the capital city, and he became known as "Yang the Invincible".

Later in his life, Yang Luchan revised *Taiji* Shadow Boxing.

He abandoned the more difficult moves in the Chen-style *Taiji Quan*, such as the high kicks, leaps and jumps, switching over to a softer and gentler style instead.

Until this day, the Yang-style *Taiji Quan* is still very popular among the wider public.

Other Sects

Martial-art novels have always revolved around the Four Major Sects, Seven Major Sects or Nine Major Sects. For instance, the Nine Major Sects include Shaolin, Wudang, Huashan, Kunlun, Diancang, Kongtong, Xueshan, Qingcheng and E'mei. In reality, these so-called sects or schools have been dramatised by novelists.

E'mei Sect 峨眉派

The E'mei Sect was supposed to have been founded by a Taoist nun in the Ming Dynasty. She fused the merits and strengths of various schools into a new form altogether, creating a set of boxing routines that combined firmness with flexibility, with a perfect balance between sham and real moves. Known as the "Jade Maiden Boxing Arts", the beautiful and graceful moves in the set were especially suitable for women.

Later on, the nun converted to Buddhism, and the Jade Maiden Boxing Arts became known as "E'mei Boxing Arts" (Mount E'mei is one of the four mountains in China sacred to Buddhism; E'mei is also the homonym of another word used to describe beautiful women). The nun began to gather female disciples widely, gradually forming the E'mei Sect. Most of the E'mei boxing routines had a feminine colour, and they had names such as "Western beauty washing her face" (*xizi xilian* 西子洗脸), "Sending the moon into hiding and flowers into shame" (*biyue xiuhua* 闭月羞花), "Wild geese fall and fishes sink" (*chenyu luoyan* 沉鱼落雁), etc. Even the sect's renowned weapon — the E'mei dagger — was inspired by and evolved from the hairpin used by women.

> There is another saying about the origins of the E'mei Sect: since ancient times, scores of Taoist priests and Buddhist monks had been making pilgrimages to the widely acclaimed Buddhist and Taoist sacred grounds in Sichuan Province, such as the monasteries and temples in E'mei and Qingcheng. These devotees would pray, meditate and recite sutras. During moments of leisure, they would even practise *wushu* routines for exercise, gradually forming an E'mei school of martial arts over the years. Thus the broadly-encompassing E'mei Sect was actually an umbrella term for all the various regional boxing styles in Sichuan Province, and most of the sect's disciples were male.

Huashan Sect 华山派

Huashan, located in Shaanxi Province, is one of the five major mountains in China. It has been said that the Hua Shadow Boxing (Hua *Quan* 华拳) was a legacy of the Huashan Sect, and became popular in the Shandong, Hebei and Shanghai areas. The so-called "Three Hua" (Three Splendours 三华) in Hua *Quan* refer to essence (*jing* 精), life force (*qi* 气) and spirit (*shen* 神), with the emphasis on "assimilating the Three Hua in One" (*san hua guan yi* 三华贯一).

Kunlun Sect 昆仑派

Legend has it that the sect's *wushu* originated from the Kunlun mountains, and later spread to He'nan, Guangdong and Guangxi. Kunlun Boxing is typically dynamic and forceful, swift and powerful, with many varied moves. It emphasises both arm and leg movements.

Kongtong Sect 崆峒派

Mount Kongtong is in Gansu Province. The only skills that were passed down from the Kongtong Sect was the Variation Boxing (*Hua Quan* 花拳)*. Variation Boxing is rich in content, and even integrates emotions — happiness, anger, sorrow and joy — into the moves.

Natural Sect 自然派

Founded by Sichuanese Shortie Xu at the end of the Qing Dynasty, the sect was given its name — Natural Sect — by Xu's heir and disciple Du Xinwu. Du had been practising a type of boxing routine named "Ghost Hand". But he felt that the name was unrefined, and changed it to "Natural Boxing". Natural Boxing focusses on building up internal qualities such as essence, spirit and life force. It is executed through a combination of feints and ambushes, with infinite, unpredictable variations that are impossible to guard against.

*The 'Hua" in Kongtong Sect's Hua Quan refers to "花", which means varied or variation. This is different from Huashan Sect's Hua 华, which means splendour.

THE BOXING ARTS

The boxing arts refer to unarmed combat. There are numerous schools of Chinese shadow boxing. Some are named after founding familes, such as the Chen-, Yang- and Wu-style *Taiji* Shadow Boxing. Others are named after the regions from which they originated, such as Shaolin and E'mei Boxing. The rest are named after animals, such as the Mantis and Monkey Boxing, and so on. Principal strokes in boxing include pushing, chopping, pulling, hooking, scooping, crushing, punching and slicing.

The Boxing Arts

Long Shadow Boxing (*chang quan* 长拳)

Long Shadow Boxing was supposedly created by the founding emperor of Song Dynasty, Zhao Kuangyin; hence it is also known as "*Taizu Quan*" (Patriarch Boxing). Long Shadow Boxing is smooth and generous in style, with movements that are nimble, swift and strong. It helps to train speed and agility, and is especially good for youths.

Eight-Trigram Boxing (*bagua zhang** 八卦掌)

This school of boxing was inspired by the Eight Trigrams, a set of symbols or codes derived from ancient Chinese metaphysical principles. Each trigram represents an object or situation. These eight trigrams can be combined into another 64 signs that represent various natural phenomena and human events. In Eight-Trigram Boxing, there are eight basic strokes, each corresponding to a trigram. Each stroke has a corresponding left and right version, hence one stroke can transform into eight forms, and the eight form into another 64 forms. In switching from one form to another, one moves quickly in circular flows, changing direction and movement constantly.

Form and Meaning Boxing (*xingyi quan* 形意拳)

Form and Meaning Boxing is derived from the Five-Element doctrine (五形思想) in Chinese philosphy. Legend has it that it was created by General Yue Fei, who lived during the Southern Song Dynasty. The basic moves in this school of boxing mirror the principles of harmony and conflict in the doctrine. At the same time, it also absorbs the style and form of 12 animals. The school of boxing is distinguished by its simple and orderly moves, which are tightly-paced, straightforward, rapid and powerful.

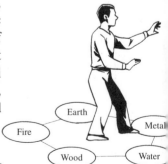

Earth

Fire

Metal

Wood

Water

* "Zhang" means "palm". This designates Bagua Zhang as a style of martial art that stresses the use of the open palm over the closed fist.

Plum Blossom Boxing (*meihua quan* 梅花拳)

Also known as Plum Blossom Pole (*meihua zhuang* 梅花桩), this school of boxing is special in that it is practised on stakes. The diameter of each stake is between three and five inches. The bottom length of the stake is driven into the ground, while the exposed top portion rises three feet and three inches above the ground.

Each stake is positioned three feet apart from front to back, and a foot and five inches apart from side to side. As one grows more skilled, one can keep raising the stakes higher above ground. Besides practising alone, one can also practise Plum Blossom Boxing with a partner, or with a group of people forming a ring on the stakes.

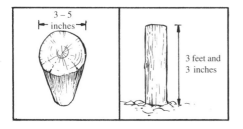

Tumbling Boxing (*ditang quan* 地趟拳)

The main characteristics of this school involve acrobatic moves such as falling, pouncing, rolling, and flipping, as well as *ditang* footwork and leg skills. Its demanding manoeuvres, such as leaping into midair and then plummeting right down, or tumbling repeatedly, often leave the audience shaking their heads in wonder. In practising each tumble and fall, one has to adhere strictly to proper instruction. Otherwise, serious injury could result from a careless slip.

Shape-shifting Boxing (*xiangxing quan* 像形拳)

Shape-shifting Boxing mimics the habits and behaviour of all sorts of animals, as well as human actions, in everyday life. They include the following examples:

- **Monkey Boxing**

  Monkey Boxing imitates the behaviour of apes and monkeys. The routine comprises the usual moves and scenarios, such as going out of the cave, peering ahead, gazing at peaches, climbing, plucking peaches, leaping from branch to branch, hiding peaches, squatting, eating peaches, returning to cave, etc. In performing the boxing routine, one must achieve suitable likeness, raising one's shoulders like a monkey, crouching down low and hunching over.

- **Snake Boxing**

  Snake Boxing emphasises restrained strength throughout the entire body, exuding gentleness on the external but imbued with great internal force. In practising the routine, one's body must tremble, the feet have to turn and swivel constantly, the two fists dodge in sudden flashes, and attacks must be bolstered by accompanying sounds, such as "heh", "hah", and "ssss".

- **Duck Boxing**

  Duck Boxing routine was inspired by how the duck emerges from water, enters water, fights for food, grooms its feathers, shakes its feathers, and other movements. In practising, one must stretch out both arms and fling them naturally, stand on tiptoe, flex the ankles, and bend both legs, kicking with either one. The body must sway back and forth, and from side to side. The routine exercises every part of the body.

- **Drunken Boxing** (*zui quan* 醉拳)

This style is often seen in *gongfu* flicks. During the Zhou Dynasty, when Duke Weiwu attempted to assassinate Prince You, he pretended to be completely plastered, staggering and stumbling in a drunken dance. Later on, the drunken mien was absorbed into martial arts and integrated closely with the moves and tactics. Gradually, Drunken Boxing emerged.

In terms of form, Drunken Boxing requires the head to nod like a series of waves, fists to swing out and strike like shooting stars, the waist to bend and sway like willow, the feet to move in broken steps and in a zig-zag path, like the Chinese character for "human" (人). In the tipsy state of staggering and lunging, one must be able to dodge and evade, yet strike through feigned guards and sudden bursts, attacking at every opportunity and striking whenever the enemy blunders.

The different routines in Drunken Boxing include "Taibai Intoxicated" (Taiba 太白 refers to Tang Dynasty poet Li Bai who loved to drink. Even when thoroughly sloshed, he was still able to write and compose poems. So others gave him the title of "Drunken Immortal"); "Tipsy Wu Song Staggers" (Wu Song is a character in *Water Margin*, one of the four great literary classics in Chinese literature. He possessed incredible strength, and could slay a tiger even when drunk); and "Eight Drunken Immortals" (eight well-loved deities in Chinese mythology).

The Story of Mantis Boxing

There was a man named Wang Lang, who lived in the period between the last days of the Ming Dynasty and the start of the Qing Dynasty. He had been deeply passionate about martial arts since childhood.

But...

Come on!

Hee!

Ha, ha!

Bang!

You've lost again!

Because of his puny size, Wang Lang always lost to his heftier senior whenever he sparred with him.

From the insect's postures, he managed to grasp manoeuvres such as sticking, dodging, hooking, pulling, locking and cutting.

He practised doggedly for three years.

One day, he sparred with his senior again.

Watch out, Senior!

Don't you ever give up?

That's fast!

The Story of Labyrinth Boxing

It is said that the budding forms of the Labyrinth Boxing (*mizong quan* 秘踪拳) first emerged during the Tang Dynasty. And when it passed into the Song Dynasty, it was further improved by Lu Junyi, chief of the Liangshan outlaws featured in *Water Margin*. He subsequently passed it to his disciple Yan Qing.

Yan Qing was a fleet-footed man, who moved as lightly as a swallow. His pugilistic skills were formidable.

Where's the man?

So people simply referred to the boxing moves he used as "Yan Qing Boxing".

One winter's day, Yan Qing ran into an imperial troop.

This Yan Qing is a rebel from Liangshan! Seize him! Quick!

Not so fast!

Those imperial dogs are sure to follow my footprints...

Heh, heh...

I'll beat them at their own game.

In a splendid display of his skills, Yan Qing created footprints of a myriad sizes, messing them up and stomping trails in different directions.

The imperial guards chased after him from morning till night...

Wait a minute!

Why are we back at the same spot? How the heck did this happen?

We must have fallen into Yan Qing's trap!

Since the incident, people started calling Yan Qing Boxing by other names, such as Lost Trail Boxing (*shizong quan* 失踪拳).

We're lost!

Hua Tuo and the Five-Animal Frolic

During the Eastern Han era, there was a medical whizz by the name of Hua Tuo (华佗). He created a set of exercises that helped to improve health and fitness, and prolong life. Called the Five-Animal Frolic (*wuqin xi*五禽戏), it is still widely popular in the martial-art world today.

For someone your age, Master, you're remarkably spritely and healthy. I've never seen you falling sick, and you walk faster than most youths. What's your secret?

Ha, ha, ha! Come with me!

He led his pupil to the front entrance of his dwelling. He opened the door gently, and then shut it softly, repeating the back and forth motions several times.

Huh?

Then he took the pupil to the storage room at the side, opening and closing the door to the room again and again.

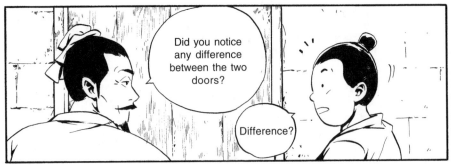

Did you notice any difference between the two doors?

Difference?

Erm... got it!

The front door swivelled more smoothly, while the side door was more jerky.

The Way to the Five-Animal Frolic

Tiger Frolic

Control your breath, lower your head, and
punch your fists like a mighty tiger.
Hands as heavy as a ton of bricks, but
don't slacken your breath.
Straighten your body, suck your *qi* to your
abdomen, then let the vital energy rise.
Feel your abdomen vibrate like thunder.
Repeat the move five or seven times.

Deer Frolic

Control your breath, lower your head,
strike like a deer.
Swivel round, and steady your body.
Suck in your tummy, arch your back,
trembling at the same time
Do it once or twice a day.

Bear Frolic

Control your breath, punch like a bear
and rear up from the side, swaggering.
Steady your stance, fill both sides of your
rib cage with *qi* and crack your joints.

Ape Frolic

Control your breath.
Be like an ape clinging to a branch, one hand
plucking a fruit, one leg swinging freely.
Raise one leg and stand on tiptoe on the other.
Turn around, circulate your *qi*, drawing it again
and again into your abdomen.

Bird Frolic

Control your breath, chin up like a
bird ready to take flight.
Direct *qi* to the top of your head, then
stretch forward like a bird in flight.

Southern Fists, Northern Legs

Southern fists

The term "southern fists, northern legs" (*nanquan beitui* 南拳北腿) is well known in the realm of martial arts. "Southern fists" refers to the southern boxing skills, which are popular in the provinces south of the Yangtze River, such as Fujian, Guangdong, Guangxi, Guizhou, Zhejiang, Hu'nan, as well as in South-east Asia. There are many schools of southern boxing, with over 100 being practised widely. Most of them have a bedazzling array of hand techniques with tightly-paced routines, powerful moves, as well as a strong emphasis on stances, and firm and solid footwork.

Northern legs

"Northern legs" refers to the schools that are popular north of the river. The northern style is exemplified by Hebei region's renowned kicking skills, in particular the Joined Kick (*lujiao* 戮脚), characterised by agile moves that deliver deadly power amid rapid and constant changes.

Routines in the Joined Kick involve both the upper and lower limbs. But the footwork is more outstanding — its particular strength lies in the unpredictable and rich variety of moves. There are more than 10 footwork routines, and over 10 kicking methods.

The Joined Kick is also known as the Mandarin Duck Kick (*yuanyang tui* 鸳鸯腿). Mandarin ducks always appear in pairs, with one leading the other. In actual combat, the two legs work together, with the left attacking and the right getting ready. Once the left leg lands, the right lifts rapidly in perfect coordination and agility.

The Invincible Kicker Du Xinwu

In the history of Chinese martial arts, there was an *wushu* exponent who possessed formidable kicking skills. His name was Du Xinwu (杜心五, 1869-1953).

Du Xinwu started learning martial arts from childhood, and was extremely talented. At the age of 12 or 13, he announced to the public his wish to seek a mentor.

Scores of adult pugilists took up the challenge, but they were all soundly trounced by the youngster.

招师

I'll hire anyone who can beat me. And I'll pay him a handsome fee.

What a scary boy! At this rate, there won't be anyone good enough to teach you!

71

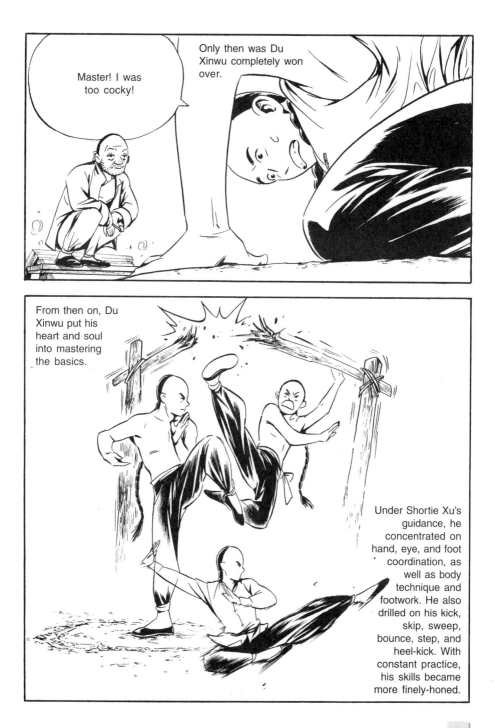

Master! I was too cocky!

Only then was Du Xinwu completely won over.

From then on, Du Xinwu put his heart and soul into mastering the basics.

Under Shortie Xu's guidance, he concentrated on hand, eye, and foot coordination, as well as body technique and footwork. He also drilled on his kick, skip, sweep, bounce, step, and heel-kick. With constant practice, his skills became more finely-honed.

Du Xinwu displayed his lightning-quick reflexes and kicking skills. He literally swept the chief of the security firm off his feet, several times in a row.

Bapp!

Ah?!

Argh!

Wow! Invincible Kicker!

So Du Xinwu became a security officer at the agency. And his fame as Invincible Kicker spread thereafter.

Bruce "Three-Legs" Lee

Bruce Lee (李小龙, 1940-1973) was a leading pugilist in the modern era. He was also a movie superstar. He founded the Jeet Kune Do 截拳道(Way of Intercepting Fist) school. His skill in the nunchaku (two-section flail) and his breathtaking kicking skills earned him worldwide fame. In fact, he was given the nickname of "Three-Legs Lee" (李三脚) for his remarkable footwork.

His early years unfolded against a backdrop of war and uncertainty.

The Japanese warplanes are coming!

But young Bruce was unfazed by the sight.

Japanese warplanes huh? You just wait and see. When I grow up, I'll gun down the whole lot of you!

Bruce! Get down quick!

You rascal! I'll skin you alive if you do this again!

Who's afraid of those Japanese planes?

Bruce's father realised that he was a hyperactive child. So when the boy turned 13, he sent him to the acclaimed Hongkong pugilist, Master Yip Mun (Ye Wen 叶问), to learn Yongchun Boxing (咏春拳), also known as Wing Chun Boxing.

Take a close look, Bruce!

As Master Yip Mun began his demonstration, each strike and move was like the wind, shadow, lightning and thunder.

I want to learn every-thing you just did!

All right, all right, but there's no hurry!

Wow! That was terrific, Master!

That was the beginning of Bruce Lee's long and lasting relationship with martial arts.

At the age of 18, Bruce Lee enrolled in the University of Washington, where he majored in philosophy.

He later opened a school in Seattle, teaching Chinese martial arts.

His fame grew. People sought him out frequently to challenge his skills.

Hordes of experts in Japanese karate, Korean taekwondo and American boxing, who came knocking on his door, limped away in utter defeat.

Once, on a street in Chinatown...

What do you think you're doing? Stop that!

Hee, hee! How dare you butt in! Get him!

Wham!

WANTED

Bong!

Bruce Lee thrashed all four of them with his bare hands, and leapt to prominence in New York City.

Upon his return to Hongkong, he started acting in movies.

Westerners have always labelled us Chinese as the "wimps of East Asia". I'm going to rid them of this notion.

I will show the whole world the courage, strength and virtue of the Chinese people.

He starred in films such as The Big Boss, Fist of Fury, and Enter the Dragon, which stirred up a worldwide craze in no time.

Aw, look! It's Three-Legs Lee!

Chinese *gongfu* is quite something! Looks like not all Chinese men are wimps!

Man! He's a god with that nunchaku!

In one of his movies, The Big Boss, Bruce Lee fought with Thai kick-boxing champion Chachai.

Chachai was known for his swift and vicious kicks. But even he was no match for Bruce Lee's triple-sweep kick!

But alas, genius is short-lived. At the age of 33, Bruce Lee died suddenly, leaving behind an eternal mystery and legend...

Bruce Lee and Jeet Kune Do
(Way of Intercepting Fist 截拳道)

Bruce Lee was not just an expert in physical manoeuvres. He also had a profound understanding of Chinese martial arts. Once, he had a duel with an acclaimed Hongkong pugilist.

Both of them used traditional *gongfu*, which turned out to be extremely awkward in actual sparring.

Lee managed to force his way to victory in the end, but he was highly dissatisfied.

He found that traditional routines were fine when it came to solo performance, but were too restrained and stylised for actual combat. It was impossible to achieve a speedy victory via the traditional way.

After much pondering and soul-searching, Bruce Lee finally abandoned fixed routines.

He created the groundbreaking styleless Jeet Kune Do, which means Way of Intercepting Fist.

Jeet Kune Do is distinguished by its speed, efficiency and emphasis on results. There are no hard and fast rules. One goes by instinct.

Because there are no fixed forms or moves in Jeet Kune Do, it can be expressed through any form or move. And therefore it is suitable for any school of martial arts.

The Pugilist's Proverbs

- Though skills may be superb, oppress not others;
  Though strength may be great, abuse not others.
- Heavier than mountains is chivalry in martial arts;
  Lighter than grass are the trappings of fame and fortune.
- The dumb bird that flies first shall emerge first from the forest;
  The dumb man who practises with diligence shall become skilful.
- Expertise in one manoeuvre is better than mere acquaintance with 1,000.
- Put virtue above all, for moral learning must grow with fighting skills.
- The defenceless should learn how to fight,
  But when they know how to fight, they should not pick fights with others.
- A pugilist does not sell his skills for even 10,000 taels of gold,
  But he will offer his skills freely at critical times.
- One must water the roots when watering plants,
  One must impart morals when imparting pugilism.
- Too tense, will break; too slow, will slack;
  Neither too tense nor too slow — now that's true skill.
- A thousand drills become a natural skill.
- Pugilism must be founded on virtue,
  Without virtue, there will be no true skill.
- A day's practice earns a day's worth of skill,
  Skip a day and waste 10 days' work.
- Let the hand be invisible from the very first strike,
  Let the opponent be unaware when the strike arrives.
- A minute on the battlefield is 1,000 days' work in the training room.
- Familiarity breeds expertise, expertise breeds creativity.
- Respect for your teachers should flow endlessly like a long stream,
  Love for your brothers should be like that of a bird feeding nestlings.
- Respect your teacher as your father.
- Let determination rule from the start of training, confidence in hard times,
  And with unending perseverance, put heart and soul into study.
- Practise *qi* internally, work the muscle, sinew and bone externally.

THE WEAPON ARTS

Weapon arts refer to the use of weaponry (arms) in martial arts. There are many types of weapons, and they can be divided largely into long weapons (spear, cudgel, pike, etc), short weapons (sabre, sword, etc), soft weapons (nine-section whip, three-section cudgel, etc) and hidden weapons. Out of the entire arms selection, the sabre and sword are the most popular. These two types of weapons are often paired up in mention, for instance: "The sabre is like a ferocious tiger, the sword like a gliding dragon".

The 18 Arts

Just what are the "18 arts"? They refer to skills in boxing and 17 weapons. The weapons are shown below:

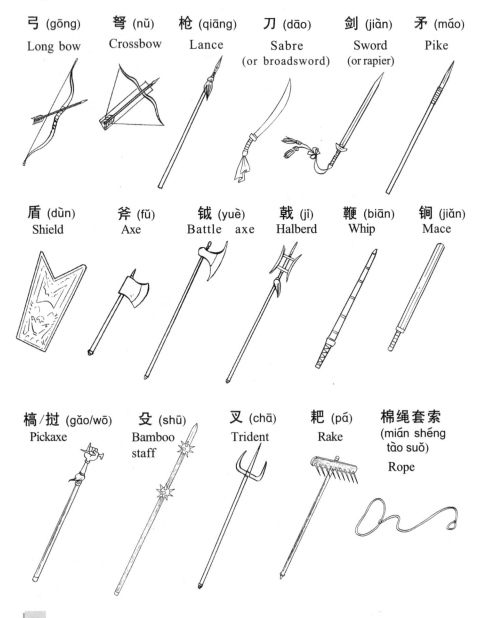

弓 (gōng)
Long bow

弩 (nǔ)
Crossbow

枪 (qiāng)
Lance

刀 (dāo)
Sabre
(or broadsword)

剑 (jiàn)
Sword
(or rapier)

矛 (máo)
Pike

盾 (dùn)
Shield

斧 (fǔ)
Axe

钺 (yuè)
Battle axe

戟 (jǐ)
Halberd

鞭 (biān)
Whip

锏 (jiǎn)
Mace

槁/挝 (gǎo/wō)
Pickaxe

殳 (shū)
Bamboo
staff

叉 (chā)
Trident

耙 (pá)
Rake

棉绳套索
(mián shéng
tào suǒ)

Rope

Sword

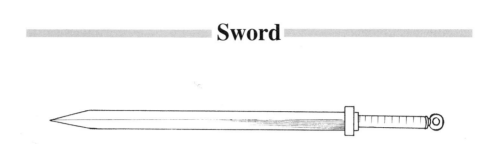

The sword or rapier (*jian* 劍) holds the elegant title of "gentleman among weapons". Throughout history, it has been a favourite with warriors, and even poets. The history of the sword can be traced back to ancient times, during the Yin-Shang era.

In the Western Zhou Dynasty, all swords were made of bronze. They were typically short, ranging between 28cm and 40cm in length. Hence usage was limited to stabbing with the sword tip. It was not feasible for other techniques such as hacking and slicing.

During the time of the Warring States, foot soldiers rose to prominence. As the main weapon of these soldiers, the sword became highly valued, and the quality of swords and swordsmanship improved. The sword became longer, and could be used to execute hacking and slicing moves.

Because bronze swords tended to be rather brittle, people began to use iron — a harder substance — to cast their swords, instead of bronze.

Double swordplay

Besides single swordplay, there is also double swordplay — wielding one sword in each hand in competition or performance.

Dagger swordplay

There is a shorter version of the sword, otherwise known as the dagger. It is suitable for close-range combat. The main moves used in dagger-play include striking, stabbing, picking, cutting and hooking.

As the dagger is short and small, it can be concealed in one's clothing and can be easily hidden from sight. For this reason, it was favoured by assassins in ancient history. One example was Zhuan Zhu, who slew King Liao of Wu State with a dagger hidden in a fish. Another was Jing Ke, who attacked Emperor Shih Huang Ti* with the same weapon.

*Founding father of Qin Dynasty

The Forging of Two Legendary Swords — Gan Jiang and Mo Xie

Gan Jiang (干将) and Mo Xie (莫邪) were two prized swords in legend. They were forged by the famous swordsmith Gan Jiang, during the Spring and Autumn Period.

Master Gan Jiang was a subject of the Wu State. One day, the king of Wu summoned him and ordered him to forge a sword.

Gan Jiang gathered the best metal and mineral ores from many famous mountains.

Husband, can we fire the furnace and start casting the sword?

We have to wait until the *yin* and *yang* elements of Heaven and Earth are in perfect harmony, when both the sun and moon shine forth at the same time, before we can begin.

The moment finally arrived. Gan Jiang started casting the sword.

Just as he was building up the fire, the weather turned chilly all of a sudden. The metal ores in the furnace would not melt.

How could this happen? This will ruin all my efforts!

Hey ho! Hey ho! Come on, everybody!

Gan Jiang roped in 300 young boys and girls to help pump the bellows and build up the fire.

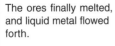

The ores finally melted, and liquid metal flowed forth.

Gan Jiang displayed his incredible skills.

He finally succeeded in casting two prized swords.

The pair — one *yin* and one *yang* — came to be known as the "Male and Female Swords".

The Male Sword was called Gan Jiang, and its blade was decorated with tortoiseshell patterns. The Female Sword was named Mo Xie, and had patterns of swirling waves.

Gan Jiang kept the *yang* sword.

He gave the *yin* sword to the king of Wu.

A white ape brandishing a tree branch lunged at her.

The village girl picked up a pole and fought back hastily.

The ape was quick and agile.

It wielded the branch with much spirit and dexterity, as if the weapon were a dancing sword.

They fought in this manner for several rounds.

The village girl kept losing. But the white ape always stopped and waited until she recovered, before they began another round.

When they grew tired, the white ape plucked some fresh fruit for her.

After they had had enough rest, the white ape picked up its branch, ready to spar again.

Your skills are too remarkable! There's no way I can beat you. Anyway, it's no fun if you keep on winning.

Why don't you teach me a couple of techniques? Then we can have another match.

The ape seemed to understand her words, and it nodded.

So the village girl copied the ape's moves and swordplay techniques. She practised thus with the ape every day, honing her skills.

Her skills became unsurpassed.

Clang!

At that time, the State of Yue was preparing to go to war against the State of Wu.

Fan Li, a senior courtier of Yue, heard about her abilities.

So he invited her to teach the soldiers in the army.

With her help, the military might of the State of Yue was greatly bolstered. Yue subsequently defeated the State of Wu.

Later generations referred to this village lass as the "Yue Maiden", and her fluid and unpredictable swordplay as the "Yue Maiden Sword" (*yuenü jian* 越女剑).

The Story of Fish Gut Sword

During the Spring and Autumn Period, there was a despotic king who ruled the Wu State.

If this goes on any further, the country will be ruined.

A nobleman, Gong Zi Guang (公子光), despised his tyranny.

His henchman Wu Zixu (伍子胥) had an idea.

The name of this warrior is Zhuan Zhu (专诸).

I know of a highly-skilled warrior. We can hire him to kill King Liao.

Gong Zi Guang took out a sword that was short and slender, but extremely sharp.

Hide this sword in the fish's stomach, ...

... until you get a chance to slay the king.

That day, Gong Zi Guang held a banquet and invited the King of Wu to feast on grilled fish.

Zhuan Zhu disguised himself as a chef and presented the grilled fish.

Don't let the assassin get away!

Kill him!

Zhuan Zhu could not fend off the onslaught single-handedly, and he fell prey to their swords.

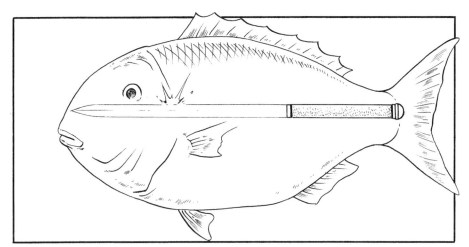

Later on, people gave the name of "Fish Gut Sword" (*yuchang jian* 鱼肠剑) to the dagger hidden in the fish's stomach.

And because the lethal stab executed by Zhuan Zhu was so accurate and powerful, it was passed down the generations, and became one of the moves in E'mei Swordplay.

E'mei Swordplay — Zhuan Zhu Slays Liao

Sabre

During the Yin-Shang era, the bronze sabre (*dao* 刀), or broadsword, had already made its appearance. And when it came to the Warring States Period, the sabre became the primary weapon for cavalry troops. Wielded from horseback, the sabre could be used to hack, split, parry, and stab — its destructive power was much greater than that of the sword or rapier. The major moves in sabre-play include splitting, hacking, lifting up, stabbing, intercepting, blocking, and more.

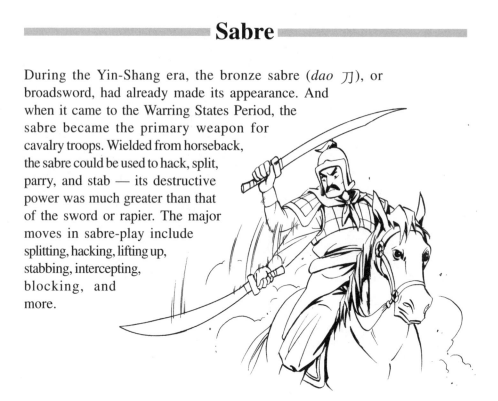

The different styles include single sabre-play, double sabre-play, and long-hilt sabre-play.

Single sabre-play

In single sabre-play, one hand wields the weapon, while the other coordinates with the sabre moves to direct or distract the opponent.

Double sabre-play

In double sabre-play, a sabre is held in each hand. The hands and the feet have to work in concert. Footwork must be agile and lively, while the sabre strokes must be clean.

Long-hilt sabre-play

The long-hilt sabre is wielded with both hands. It is a grand, powerful and deadly weapon, and was often used in ancient times by military generals on horseback.

In the literary classic *Romance of the Three Kingdoms*, the "Green Dragon on Moon Sabre" wielded by Duke Guan is one example of a renowned long-hilt sabre. Sabre play typically displays ferocious, swift and powerful moves.

Yang Zhi Sells His Sabre

Of the 108 outlaws in the literary classic *Water Margin*, there was one named Yang Zhi (杨志), whose martial skills were unsurpassed. The story of how he tried to sell his sabre is particularly well known.

Yang Zhi used to be an imperial guard, until a mishap happened. He was accompanying a shipment of rare plants and precious stones when a strong wind capsized the ship.

Yang Zhi did not dare return to the court, so he fled to the far ends of the land.

* Each string has 1,000 cash coins.

Yang Zhi could not stand it anymore. In one stroke, he killed Niu Er.

I'll take full responsibility for what I've done. I'll give myself up to the magistrate right now.

But the entire neighbourhood was grateful to Yang Zhi for getting rid of Niu Er the great pest, so they volunteered to be witnesses at the magistrate's court.

Thank you for getting rid of Hairy Beast!

Lance

The lance (*qiang* 枪) is considered the king of weapons, because in ancient times, it was often wielded by generals and military commanders.

The lance shaft is fashioned from a special wood from the Chinese ash, which is pliable and has an elastic quality. This ensures that after the lance is bent in a powerful thrust, throw or blow, it can bounce back to its original shape.

In ancient times, the lance was known as the spear (*mao* 矛), and was used as early as the reign of the Yellow Emperor*. It was an important weapon on the battlefield, especially for mounted fighters. Compared to shorter weapons such as the sabre or rapier, the lance was much easier to manoeuvre from horseback, and was more effective in striking fatal blows to the enemy.

The lance moves in a wide and open style, flipping and flying up and down in an unpredictable slew of strokes. It can extend out or retreat without warning, and usually focusses on a particular point of attack. Hence there is the saying: "the lance thrusts in a straight line".

* *Legendary ruler and ancestor of the Chinese nation.*

One Stroke Victory

During the Qing Dynasty, there was a man in Hebei Province named Wu Zhong. He started learning martial arts from a young age, and by adulthood, was an expert in all fields, whether in bare-fist boxing or the weapon arts.

Many youths came knocking on his door, begging him to teach them.

One day, Wu Zhong was teaching lance work to his students on the field.

A bunch of curious onlookers gathered nearby.

Among them was an elderly couple.

This is the routine known as 108 Lances. Watch closely!

Wu Zhong's lance danced in a hundred different ways, dazzling the eyes of the onlookers.

Master Wu is incredible with the lance!

Amazing! Terrific!

Superb!

God of Lance! God of Lance!

Wu Zhong felt very pleased with himself.

Oh, it's nothing much. You're too kind.

At this moment, the elderly couple walked up to him.

The old man saw that Wu Zhong was sincere, so he agreed.

Wu Zhong invited the elderly couple to stay in his home, treating them with utter respect.

Does he have to do that?

Well, you started it by showing off.

The old man taught Wu Zhong all his consummate skills — the Eight Ultimate Boxing and Six Combination Lance Play.

Wu Zhong's skills improved tremendously, especially in lance play, for which he earned the nickname of "God of Lance".

Now I'm truly the God of Lance!

Staff

Like the lance, the staff (*gun* 棍) is made of Chinese ash wood as well.

The staff is also a very ancient weapon. It is simple to make, and the earliest version of it was probably a natural stick or branch, or something similar that had undergone slight modifications.

During the prehistoric era, Mankind already knew how to wield the staff against wild beasts, using it to defend themselves, or even to pick and gather food, and catch fish.

In staff play, both ends of the weapon are used in combat. The strokes flow continuously and densely, with vicious power and great variety in style. Therefore there is a martial-art proverb that says: "the staff strikes everywhere".

The Scholar Teaches Staff Play

Towards the end of the Ming Dynasty, there was a scholar named Zhu Ya (朱崖).

Scholar Zhu was a talented man, well-versed in the literary arts as well as martial arts, where his specialty was staff play.

The staff should be wielded with great force... like this... and like that...

One day, he noticed a group of warriors and pugilists discussing the art of staff play.

Well then, let me give you a taste of what I know!

I'll take care of this arrogant fool!

But no matter how swiftly or slowly the man thrust, all his attacks were parried by the cool and collected Scholar Zhu.

In the end, Scholar Zhu knocked him off his feet with one blow of the staff.

With eyes agog and jaws dropped, the pugilists and fighters listened intently to every word of the scholar. They were completely won over.

Now in combat, so long as you concentrate and hold on firmly to your staff, your defence will be impenetrable and your attacks successful. Using brute force will only waste your strength. And once your strength starts to fail, you will lose concentration. Then defeat will be certain.

Soft Weapons

Three-section flail 三节棍 （sān jié gùn）
Thethree-section flail is a type of soft weapon, made
by linking three sections of Chinese ash wood with
lengths of iron chain. Usually, one flail-section is
held in each hand. Main moves include rotating,
sweeping and splitting. The instrument is highly
portable. In usage, it can advance or retreat, extend
or retract, and is highly flexible and unpredictable.

Nine-section whip 九节鞭 （jiǔ jié biān）
Thenine-section whip is another type of soft weapon.
It can be concealed completely when stuffed in the
hand, but when lashed out, unfurls into a whip as
long as a human body. Like the three-section flail, it
can also be short or long. It makes a whooshing
sound in motion, and can be wielded to create a
rich variety of moves.

Shooting star rope 流星锤 （liú xīng chuí）
Theshooting star rope is also a soft weapon. It has
a long history that goes back to ancient times. Then,
people would fasten a rock to a strip of creeper or
vine, forming a "flying-rock rope". During hunts,
they would fling these cords at the wild beasts to
trip them, trussing up their four limbs. These flying-
rock ropes were the precursors to the shooting star
rope. There are two forms of this weapon: the single-
star rope, and the double-star rope.

Secret Weapons

Secret weapons are great for catching opponents unawares.

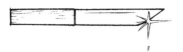

Flying dagger (*feidao* 飞刀)
A kind of hand-thrown weapon.
About 20cm long.

Flying dart (*feibiao* 飞镖)
Also a hand-thrown weapon.
About 10cm long.

Plum blossom needle (*meihua zhen* 梅花针)
Another hand-thrown device, comprising five needles, each about 5cm in length, fused together at the bottom. The device pierces its target in five spots, marking it with a pattern rather like a five-petal plum blossom.

Sleeve arrow (*xiujian* 袖箭)
A shooting device that works by ejecting a short arrow from inside a shirtsleeve, using the mechanical action of springs.

Flying claw (*feizhao* 飞爪)
A type of rope device, with a sharp, claw-like instrument attached. Can be used to lasso or injure a person.

Blood spilling weapon (*xue dizi* 血滴子)
Also a kind of rope device. Sharp, thin blades are attached to the ring of a lasso. The lasso is thrown around the victim's head, and then tightened until the spinning blades slice off the head.

My head!

Miscellaneous Terms

Set pattern (*taolu* 套路)

This refers to a *gongfu* routine. A complete set pattern comprises 20, 30, or even up to 100 series of moves. In a boxing routine, a fist often strikes out then draws in. This to-and-fro movement is referred to as "a trip". Set patterns are divided into boxing and weapon routines.

Stances (*zhama* 扎马)

One poses in a particular stance for 15 minutes, then rests for five minutes, before moving on to another stance.

Pole exercises (*zhuanggong* 桩功)

Pole exercises are part of the basic training in martial arts. During practice, one must hold still like a standing pole, while adjusting and regulating one's *qi* flow. This will build up internal power.

Seizing (*qinna* 擒拿)

No weapons are used in seizing. Using bare hands, one strikes or locks the opponent's joints, acupoints, and other key areas, rendering him immobile so that he can be seized easily. This is one of the four tenets of martial combat, which include kicking, striking, throwing and seizing.

Hand blocking (*lanshou* 拦手)

This means using various hand techniques to block the opponent's attacks. These techniques emphasise flexibility and moves such as winding around, thrusting, hooking, chopping, blocking, intercepting and holding. Each move is executed with a spinning or turning motion, and is vigorous and powerful.

THE ETHICS OF CHINESE MARTIAL ETHICS

Martial ethics or chivalry (*wude* 武德) is highly prized in the world of martial arts. There are many adages on the subject. Some examples include "Heavier than mountains is chivalry in martial arts; lighter than grass are the trappings of fame and fortune"; "Virtue is top priority in martial arts", "Aspiring pugilists should first master the code of ethics", etc.

Why this fixation with chivalry? This is because martial arts gives its practitioners an edge over other common folk. A virtuous pugilist could benefit his fellow men, but an unscrupulous one could well turn out to be a great scourge of the common people.

Song of Chivalry

Be proper in aim, keep strong and healthy, and defend the nation;
Be upright in conduct, exercise humility and caution, train body and soul;
Be strong in will, do good and forsake evil, look always to the light;
Be industrious in learning, never let loose your fist, practise through day and night;
Be proficient in skill, practice makes perfect, and skill breeds courage;
Be strict in discipline, do not attack ruthlessly, and stick to the rules;
Be kind in teaching, love your disciple, teach him virtue as well as skill;
Be virtuous in morals, revere your teacher and the Way, respect both old and young.

Martial rituals

Rituals are also a part of martial ethics. Hence during a *wushu* match, we see contestants offering a fist-salute to their opponent, before they begin sparring. One hand is clenched into a fist, while the other palm wraps over it.

This simple fist-salute is actually highly meaningful.

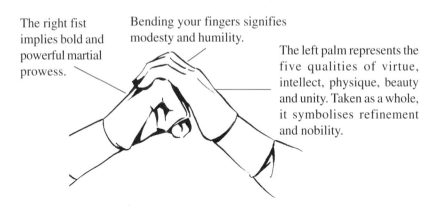

The right fist implies bold and powerful martial prowess.

Bending your fingers signifies modesty and humility.

The left palm represents the five qualities of virtue, intellect, physique, beauty and unity. Taken as a whole, it symbolises refinement and nobility.

The left palm represents culture and civility, the right fist military might. A true exponent of martial arts is a master of both pen and sword, and remains a humble student at heart.

Wrapping the left palm over the right fist denotes restraint, and controlled power.

By bringing the left palm and right fist together with your arms circled, it means that you embrace the whole world as your home, offer your humble cooperation, and seek a kindred spirit through friendly sparring.

Gan Fengchi Teaches Iron Head a Lesson

The pugilist Gan Fengchi (甘凤池) was a folk hero in the Jiangnan region, who lived during the Qing Dynasty. He was generous and warm-hearted, and despised villains. He was an expert in both the external and internal schools of martial arts. Because of his peerless skills, people gave him the nickname "Invincible Gan".

Oh dear! These two bulls are blocking the road! When are they going to stop tussling?

One day...

I'm in a hurry to get into the city!

With his bare hands, Gan Fengchi grabbed the bulls by the horns. He gave each of them a shove, pushing them onto either side of the road.

143

Iron Head took a few steps back. Then he charged with all his might towards Gan Fengchi's stomach.

The force of the recoil sent him tumbling backwards, and he sprained his wrist.

To his shock, it was as if he had bounced off a big rubber ball.

Ouuuuuch!

Would you like another try?

Spare me, Master Gan! I was too full of myself!

Come on, get up!

Remember this — a pugilist must always be chivalrous. On no account should he use his powers to oppress others. There will always be someone else bigger and better than you.

Here, this medicine is for your injury.

Not only was Gan Fengchi highly-skilled, he was also a compassionate man who lived up to his reputation as a folk hero. He was respected by all, and left a good name for posterity.

Basic Exercises

Basic exercises lay the foundation for martial-art skills. There are many different types of such exercises, some of which are shown below:

Leg Exercises

1. Leg presses

a) Front press   b) Back press   c) Side extension squat

2. Leg pulls

a) Front pull   b) Side pull   c) Back pull

3. Splits

a) Forward split   b) Lateral split

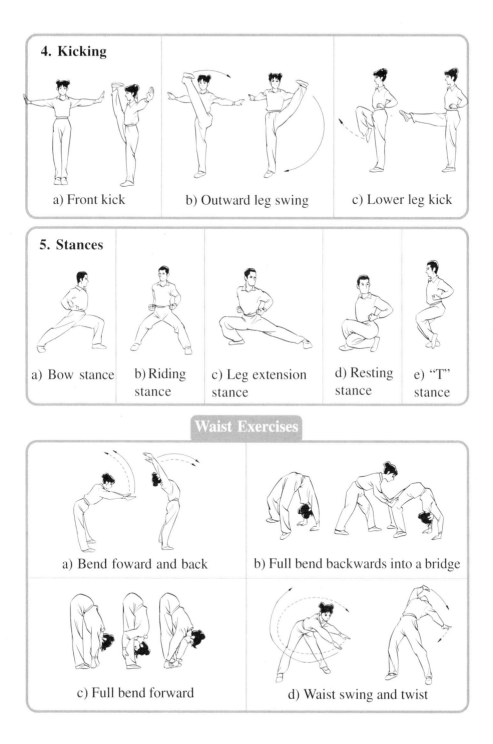

4. Kicking

a) Front kick

b) Outward leg swing

c) Lower leg kick

5. Stances

a) Bow stance

b) Riding stance

c) Leg extension stance

d) Resting stance

e) "T" stance

Waist Exercises

a) Bend foward and back

b) Full bend backwards into a bridge

c) Full bend forward

d) Waist swing and twist

Shoulder Exercises

a) Shoulder press

b) Arms swing in full circle

Jumping Exercises

a) Flying kick

b) Front swing leap

Balancing Exercises

a) Swallow balance

b) Leg-tuck balance

c) Knee-raise balance

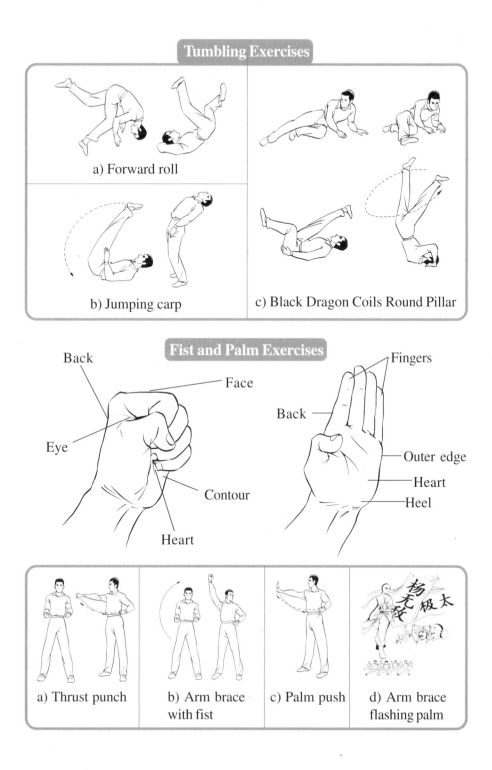

Tumbling Exercises

a) Forward roll

b) Jumping carp

c) Black Dragon Coils Round Pillar

Fist and Palm Exercises

Back

Face

Eye

Contour

Heart

Fingers

Back

Outer edge

Heart

Heel

a) Thrust punch

b) Arm brace with fist

c) Palm push

d) Arm brace flashing palm

A Brief Chronology of Chinese History

夏 Xia Dynasty			About 2100 – 1600 BC
商 Shang Dynasty			About 1600 – 1100 BC
周 Zhou Dynasty	西周 Western Zhou Dynasty		About 1100 – 771 BC
	東周 Eastern Zhou Dynasty		770 – 256 BC
	春秋 Spring and Autumn Period		770 – 476 BC
	戰國 Warring States		475 – 221 BC
秦 Qin Dynasty			221 – 207 BC
漢 Han Dynasty	西漢 Western Han		206 BC – AD 24
	東漢 Eastern Han		25 – 220
三國 Three Kingdoms	魏 Wei		220 – 265
	蜀漢 Shu Han		221 – 263
	吳 Wu		222 – 280
西晉 Western Jin Dynasty			265 – 316
東晉 Eastern Jin Dynasty			317 – 420
南北朝 Northern and Southern Dynasties	南朝 Southern Dynasties	宋 Song	420 – 479
		齊 Qi	479 – 502
		梁 Liang	502 – 557
		陳 Chen	557 – 589
	北朝 Northern Dynasties	北魏 Northern Wei	386 – 534
		東魏 Eastern Wei	534 – 550
		北齊 Northern Qi	550 – 577
		西魏 Western Wei	535 – 556
		北周 Northern Zhou	557 – 581
隋 Sui Dynasty			581 – 618
唐 Tang Dynasty			618 – 907
五代 Five Dynasties	後梁 Later Liang		907 – 923
	後唐 Later Tang		923 – 936
	後晉 Later Jin		936 – 946
	後漢 Later Han		947 – 950
	後周 Later Zhou		951 – 960
宋 Song Dynasty	北宋 Northern Song Dynasty		960 – 1127
	南宋 Southern Song Dynasty		1127 – 1279
遼 Liao Dynasty			916 – 1125
金 Jin Dynasty			1115 – 1234
元 Yuan Dynasty			1271 – 1368
明 Ming Dynasty			1368 – 1644
清 Qing Dynasty			1644 – 1911
中華民國 Republic of China			1912 – 1949
中華人民共和國 People's Republic of China			1949 –

CHINESE CULTURE SERIES
150x210mm, fully illustrated

ORIGINS OF CHINESE PEOPLE AND CUSTOMS
Explores the beginnings of the Chinese people, origins of Chinese names, Chinese zodiac signs, the afterlife, social etiquette and more!

ORIGINS OF CHINESE FESTIVALS
Stories about Lunar New Year, Chinese Valentine's Day, Qing Ming, Dragon Boat, Zhong Yuan, Mid-Autumn Festivals and more.

ORIGINS OF CHINESE CULTURE
Interesting facts about the "Four Treasures of the Study": the brush, ink, paper and inkstone, which form the cornerstone of Chinese culture.

ORIGINS OF CHINESE MARTIAL ARTS
Traces the origins of the *gongfu* of Shaolin and Wudang warriors and their philosophy and chivalry code.

ORIGINS OF SHAOLIN KUNG FU
An entertaining read for all budding martial arts enthusiasts and all who want to explore the wonders of Shaolin Kung Fu!

ORIGINS OF CHINESE CUISINE
Showcases famous and best-relished dishes, including Peking Roast Duck and Buddha Jumps Over the Wall, and the stories behind them.

ORIGINS OF CHINESE FOOD CULTURE
Covers the origins, history, customs, and the art and science of Chinese food culture, including the 18 methods of cooking.

ORIGINS OF CHINESE TEA AND WINE
Tea and wine have a long history in China. In fact, both have become firmly entrenched in the culture and customs of the Chinese people.

ORIGINS OF CHINESE SCIENCE & TECHNOLOGY
Covers great inventions by the Chinese: the compass, paper-making, gunpowder and printing. Also explores Chinese expertise in the fields of geography, mathematics, agriculture and astronomy.

***NEW:* Origins of Chinese Art & Craft; Origins of Chinese Names**

中华武术的故事

绘画 ：张开振
翻译 ：晖 子

亚太图书有限公司出版